Level Up! The Guide

How to turn your ideas into your business!

B. Marie Blaine

Level Up! The Guide
How to turn your ideas into your business!

Introduction-

Preplanning

Today is the beginning of your new endeavor! Today is the day you start planning your new business. This book was written to be a guide to help you start your business step by step. Throughout the years, I have had many meetings of the minds and many ideas people have consulted with me on that have not happened due to various reasons. When it came down to the core reason people don't pursue their business idea, it was because of lack of support and fear of failure. Afraid of making mistakes and not taking the right steps.
Have you dreamed of starting a business and don't know where to start? Have you already started and want to make this a full-time career? Have you been in business and need to incorporate in order to take your business to the

next level? This guide is for you! I decided to create a guide that can assist you step by step. This guide is also supported by a team that you can reach out to any time and call for support. More information about support services will be covered later. I want you to reach your dreams and make them a reality. Many people think it can't happen, but it can! This book is going to cover each necessary step to start your business.

    I am a financial consultant and accountant that works with a team of accountants that have assisted many businesses in starting and getting successfully up and running. This guide was developed to ease the process for entrepreneurs. This book is my gift to you that will walk you through starting your business step by step.

    Personal support services are available to provide one on one direction as well. This book includes the necessary steps to start your business. Your business can be developed and up and running by the end, as the chapters give a firm outline of needed information for your business. This guide will help you see a timeline as far as true growth in your business.

Confidence is a foundational tool in starting anything. If you believe that you are not capable of the task you will focus on the hurdles instead of the goal. This is a necessary tool for you to get to the next step in the process. Some will fake it until they make it, but how far does faking it really get you? It may truly get us a lot further than we think it can. If you're not confident about speaking, find something you are confident in. Usually, if we are skilled at something we have no problem talking about it. Ask me about Politics, I don't have much to say. However, ask me about finance and we can talk about it for hours. Humans tend to speak more comfortably about things that they know or they have researched. Why do we lack confidence? What are we ashamed of or what are we hiding? Can you look in the mirror and honestly say nothing? No! Is there anyone who can say no? So, now why do you lack confidence again? Every single person you speak to has a story. Every single person you converse with has something you don't know. Even your own mother. So why are you lacking confidence again? Be bold in what you say, be strong in what you do. Master your practice! Be Confident!..... -Brooke's Thoughts

Every day I run into someone who wants to start a business. I run into these future entrepreneurs in business meetings, restaurants, markets, in the park, taking a stroll, etc. Pretty much your fellow small business owner can be sitting next to you while you are reading this book. Businesses come from ideas and almost everyone has at least one. You may have started your business and are looking to take it to the next level or you may be starting from scratch. In either position, you're pushing forward. Congratulations for taking the first step! You're showing work ethic, determination, and courage. The first step to creating your business is what you are already doing preplanning. Planning helps you create a step by step process for success. Let's take all of those awesome ideas going thru your head and write them down. We are going to start with the bare necessities. In the following chapters, we will brush over the who, what where, when, why and how of your business. We will then go into detail in later chapters. What is your idea? Do you have a name for your business? What industry?

Upon completion of this book, my goal is to have your business up and running. Only 20% of businesses survive the first five years. If you have already made it over the five-year hump congratulations. Let's help you expand!

Keep your workbook close as you read this book, we will fill out the workbook as we go along. The number one thing that stops people from starting businesses is fear. Top three excuses people give are; lack of money, lack of time, and lack of knowledge. All of those 'Excuses' can be eliminated. What is stopping you? Please write this down.

Let's start your business!

Chapter 1

Who is a part of this company?

These are two of the most paralyzing emotions known to man. They can keep you from even trying to accomplish your dreams and desires. They can defuse your thought process and erode your confidence. Although they are both rooted in the same emotion they are nourished by different outcomes. They both result in settling for mediocrity. They are Fear of Failure and Fear of Success. Many of us fear the embarrassment of failure but there are also those who fear the responsibility of success. And fear is simply lack of self-confidence. But we have all stood up to fear at some point and taken action in spite of the situation. What enabled you to take that stand? It's simply that you perceived the outcome of not taking action much more undesirable than the outcome of taking action. The next time you think you can't, ask yourself, "Do I fear failure or do I fear success"? Because I believe there is nothing you can't-do, only things that you will not put forth the effort to accomplish. And you will not put forth the effort if you don't value the outcome as worthy of the required action. When you stand up to a bully they will generally go away. When you stand up to fear it dissipates and disappears.- Blaine Group Moments

Who is going to be a part of this business? If you plan to be a sole proprietor, you will still need people that assist you in making this business successful. This can be someone you need to simply support your service or someone you need to create the website or do marketing etc.

In this chapter I want you to think about who you are going to need to support your business if you don't plan on having any partners. I personally have IT, marketing, development support and a few others. Mainly people who may specialize in an area I don't know much about. These people are not partners they are only contractors and much needed support to make my business successful. I want you to look at your workbook and answer the first question.

Go to your workbook to answer question 1 for Chapter 1.

Professional services can be many things this can be lawyers, financial consulting, business consultants, IT consultants, security consultants, marketing guru's, salesman, etc. There are many different professional services your business can take advantage of to enhance the business. Enhancing the business is key. If you want your business to grow, you must analyze the value in hiring a professional vs. doing it yourself. I am a firm believer of doing things myself, so sometimes, I will complete them myself and then pay the professional to review. They will usually complete the review at a lower cost because they are not completing the task.

Partners

If you are going to have multiple owners of the business things can become complicated. Setup with multiple owners is key.

Go to your workbook to answer question 2-5 for Chapter 1.

These are only a few of the questions you must consider if you are going to have multiple owners. I suggest having a Partnership agreement setup that does not only identify 50/50 but it addresses the time each partner is to put in the business each week, withdrawals, leaving the partnership, adding new partners, distribution of profits and losses, retained profit, borrowing money, etc. This is only the beginning of the important questions that have to be answered when forming a partnership.

Very often with partnerships or multiple owners, one ends up completing the grunt of the work, however, the profit split is equal. If there is an active owner versus an inactive owner and you all plan to split the profit due to the original investment, great, however, pay the active partner a salary on top of the split. When we are talking 50/50 in the business world, in all fairness it should truly be 50/50, however, it is usually not.

Remember when you incorporate your business, someone will be identified as the President, Treasurer and the Secretary. These are not even roles if each of these officers is a partial owner, the split, and work expected to be completed by the owner should be written in an agreement. Many have told me that the person is their friend and there is no reason for all the extra paperwork. If this person is your friend, even more, the reason why you both should want the company set-up properly so you both can be protected. I truly don't recommend any partnership agreements or multiple-owner organizations be established without a lawyer. You are opening this company to make money, right? So why would you start as if it is going to take you 20 years to make substantial money? Set yourself up properly from the start.

I had a client, Bob, who said he wanted to start this company with a partner, Joe, and the split was going to be 50/50. I suggested that they write a partnership agreement, even if they didn't include a lawyer draw out the 50/50 specifics. They, of course, rebutted telling me they had been good friends for such a long time and they wouldn't need to have such agreement in place. The business started off well, however, Joe was indebted to his 9-5, working 9-9 and was unable to invest as much time as Bob. The business started off well, they were making a profit and they kept to their split of profits and losses being 50/50. Eventually, Bob had an accident in the facility that resulted in an insurance increase for the company. They still worked things out and came up with a verbal agreement for Bob to pay a higher percentage of the insurance increase due to the loss. The business continued to run and the partner stuck to their agreement. Now Joe has an accident on the property as well and the insurance sky rockets again causing the business to close, this time. Who takes the loss or do they take it 50/50? Well, Joe wanted to take it 50/50, however, Bob paid his higher portion and did not. Here is the issue. How do Bob and Joe decide who to split the loss? Here is the solution. This could have been avoided with a partnership that sticks to the rules agreed upon.

I tell you this story because businesses ruin friendships and relationships all the time. Instead of taking the risk of ruining a relationship. Write a proper Partnership agreement.

Board of Directors

Your board of directors most of the time is a group that funded the business but does not work in it. If someone in your board of directors operates the business they should have a salary separate of their split. Every officer should have the split and responsibility specified in terms. Each director should have a position if possible and if not. The terms need to include any compensation or stipend that will be given for fulfilling the officer position each year. The law of election of officers as well as, adds and withdrawals of the board should be specified.

When members of partnership or board are assigned and the value of each person should be noted. The credentials and value that they bring to the company should be specified and even valued if possible. It is important to know the value of each person, as far as what they bring to the table to help your team make fair partnership decisions. All licenses and certifications should be in their file as they may be able to be used in the future even if they are not currently of value. Many companies have also implemented psychological evaluations. These evaluations give you psychological warnings about the party you are going into business and may also be considered as well.

Chapter 2

Mission, Vision, and Values

When you reach your goal, no matter how big or small, don't stop. It took effort, drive, endurance, perseverance, integrity, and so many other qualities to accomplish what you set out to do. Why let those qualities sit idle. Find your next plateau. Frank Lloyd Wright was asked, late in his life, which of his accomplishments did he consider his greatest? His answer, the next. What is your next? Use those qualities to be more, to do more. No matter how exhausting the journey, the exhilaration of your accomplishment is always worth the effort. And all the time you were working, and praying, and building yourself up, someone was watching, and being inspired. Everything that you have experienced has been watched and dissected, and analyzed, by someone you are not aware of. In the same way, you looked at someone and said, if they can do it, I can do it, someone is watching you. There are others like you, who are looking for the opportunity but may not have the self-confidence. They will gain that confidence by watching you. There are others who may lack specific knowledge, but they will learn from your mistakes. There are others who are like you were when you made your first step and will make their first step because you did. If you have succeeded at anything, great or small, you are an inspiration to someone else. Keep growing, keep expanding, keep challenging yourself. For the world to become better, we have to become better. For the world to change, we have to change. For the world to see the possible, someone has to do the impossible. What's next for you? - Blaine Group Moments

Go to your workbook and answer questions 1-3 for Chapter 2.

Another very important part of planning is giving the purpose of your business. This should be a short blurb that encompasses the reason you are in business. Your purpose should lead into how you are going to run this business and be successful.

Ex. We are in business to provide meals to the local low-income community members that lack food to eat.

From this purpose, I can tell you what the business does. I can't tell how it runs, however, this sentence can also lead well into the how explanation.

Ex. We will provide food to families by accepting donations from local restaurants and companies. We will then prepare food and serve it to all families that attend dinners.

The first step is to write your purpose. It should be more than one sentence the more details the better. No more than two-three sentences for your incorporation documents. For company bylaws, you can write more. You won't give the full purpose when you incorporate, however you should include enough detail for a general overview. Your statement should be able to answer general questions you may receive. A complete purpose will lead into a complete how explanation. I recommend that your how-to explanation is detailed a minimum of a page. Your how explanation is the beginning of your policies and procedures guide. Include as many details as possible, this will give you a stronger basis for your policies and procedures guide.

Are you thinking, why do I need a policy and procedures guide? A guide of this nature structures your company and the way you make money. It gives your employees a basis when you need to hire. It creditworthiness and creates a process to your success. A documented process that can be updated. When you have the steps written out it is easier to change them to make them better. You give yourself the ability to identify where the issues occur and how they can be changed or improved without changing the rest of the process.

Everything in this book will be a step towards something else that will need to be completed in your business in order to be successful. The key to my processes is that they complete a part but they also begin something else. Why not get two things done at once? Instead of one.

Go to your workbook to answer questions 4-5 for Chapter 2.

With these descriptions being complete, let's move on and address your mission and vision statement. Your mission is your company goal, this can also be updated yearly or whenever key officers agree that it should. Your mission should encompass what your company plans to achieve by operating this business. For example, you have a t-shirt company that sells inspirational shirts. Your mission may be, 'to inspire and impact the community in a positive way by selling shirts that inspire those around us and carry positive messages in the form of shirts'. Yes, I took something as simple as selling a t-shirt and made it a small motivational speech you can do this too. A barber's vision can be to uplift the community by making men and boys feel good about themselves and teach them about grooming in the absence of their fathers.

Your mission is a summary of your purpose and how-to statement. I want you to think about Walmart. Do you know their mission and vision? Their mission is to give people access to better lives by helping them save money. The mission of this book is to help improve lives in the community by showing them they are able to start a business with what is in their hands.

Go to your workbook to answer question 6 for Chapter 2.

Where do you see your company in 5- 10 years? Do you plan on doing anything philanthropic? Do you have a plan to be able to support a specific cause? Do you just want your business to be a sales powerhouse? Your company's vision is where you see the company going or how you see the company affecting the community it is servicing in the years to come. My vision for this book is to be able to support has many small business entrepreneurs as possible. I want to help people start their business and make the process simple. I want to provide a guide that will become a go-to for people all around the world that want to start their own business. Yes, there are some more pieces to this vision than this book, however, that is the direction in which I'm heading.

Go to your workbook to answer questions 7 for Chapter 2. Make both statements 2-3 sentences no more than 5. These statements should be brief and to the point. The reader should be able to fully understand your intent. Make sure your explanation includes important details.

Remember your mission and vision is an intro to your company. Take a little time to work on this. One of the first things that your consumer is going to look at on your website is going to be your mission and vision statements. Prospective consumers want to know what your company is about and what they are looking to achieve. The service you provide may pull the client in, yet your mission and vision will make your client committed.

Go to your workbook to answer questions 8-9 for Chapter 2.

Chapter 3

Location, location, location

Is thinking rehashing the past, or preparing to create a future? Is how we think and what we think about a learned response? Is thinking daydreaming or strategizing? For each of us, thinking has a different nuance, a different concept. For many, thinking is a bore, time spent with no immediate outcome. But for others, it is a necessity before taking the ...next step. What we think about thinking is a direct consequence of how we see ourselves. If you see yourself as resourceful, you will think resourceful thoughts. If you see yourself as a victim, your thoughts will be fearful and powerless. For the vast majority of us, our thinking is an automatic response and we find ourselves sad, or discouraged because that is our thought pattern. We don't have to stay in those patterns, but we first have to think and identify our thoughts. When you think about your goals do you see hard work and difficulty, or do you see everything coming together? The primary thing that separates the successful entrepreneur from a homeless person is how they think, more precisely how they think about themselves. The homeless person has given up hope, they may be college educated and have been an executive on Wall Street, but they've lost their will, while the successful entrepreneur has overcome countless hopeless situations. Change your thinking. See your goals as stepping stones, your dreams as a reality. But to get a better outcome you've got to think better about yourself, about who you are, and about what you are capable of. - Blaine Group Moments

During the planning of your company, you must decide where your company will conduct business. Many folks are considering an online option which is great and reduces overhead. This also enables a quick start. Food trucks are also very popular in the Charlotte area and have become a better option instead of opening a retail location for restaurant owners, in the beginning. I agree that a temporary option with minimal cost may be the way you want to start your business. However, I recommend that you list out all of your pros and cons. Location is very important.

Go to your workbook to answer question 1 for Chapter 3.

Physical
    If you decide your business needs a physical location, great. The next decision will be where. Now your market comes into play with this decision. Along with choosing a physical location that will be conducive to business, you want to choose a location that is accessible and appealing to your clientele. Your choice of location can limit your clients.
    Physical locations come with a few more complications than online, first one being where

do you want your storefront or office. This is very important because you want to make sure your location is within reach for your target client. If parking is not available this will affect your traffic, depending on the traffic you are looking to attract. When you are deciding your physical location, make a list of requirements. Then take that list and order them with the highest priority first. If you own a home unless it was custom built you settled without having some of the things you would have liked to have. Same thing here, make sure your first five requirements are met. Whatever is not available, do research to see how you can fulfill the need in other ways.

Depending on where you are in town, clients may not want to travel to the other side of town or may not feel comfortable coming from the other side of town. If you have bus riders as clientele, a location close to public transportation may be a requirement. Other factors you may want to consider when deciding your location is traffic make sure the street is not too busy. Too busy or no parking may deter those that need to park and don't have much time. If you want to attract women, I wouldn't' necessarily set up my business in an industrial or secluded area. Secluded areas may have women weary to visit after dusk. Women usually want to feel safe at the businesses they patronize. My personal motto is always put yourself in the mind of your customer.

Go to your workbook to answer question 2 for Chapter 3.

Online
     Lately, most entrepreneurs are taking advantage of the online option however, you must have a marketing plan in place to create traffic. This YouTube should include a free giveaway to attract people. Items to sell or service to sell. You must give your audience a taste to create the desire for your business. As with physical locations, online services and sales have base cost. Some base cost you should

consider is your cost of sales. This may include your website, hosting, advertising, card services, etc. This is just the beginning of cost for your online business. There will be an additional cost based on the nature of your business, however, with online services, this is where you should begin.

Marketing is very important online. You must find a way to drive traffic to your site. Facebook is an excellent marketing tool and has actually been one of the top places to advertise over the last few years. Google AdWords is also at the top of the list. You can start your advertising on your own, however, if you're not willing to complete the research call someone who specializes in this field. We will address marketing in depth in the next chapter.

Go to your workbook to answer question 3 for Chapter 3.

The presentation is also very important. Be careful when building your website or have someone build it for you. Always make sure all of your links are functioning. Make sure the site is appealing to the eye of your target market. For example, if you desire to have a primarily female audience, your site should have a feminine touch. Maybe a gray base with highlights of a soft pink. Just an idea. If you're offering a professional service, make sure it is professional.

Apps are also key these days as people want things as fast as possible. So if your service can work thru an app, why not. You make your business is more accessible and a go-to for your desired client.

Along with your location comes telephone and email contact. Set these up, you can set them up for free to start off with. Google voice is popular and Sideline is awesome as well. You can change things over to a paying option when you earn revenue to cover the cost. Don't put yourself in unnecessary debt if you don't have definite predictions as to when money is going to start coming in. Establish yourself first.

Chapter 4

Who is your Target Market?

Today my first thoughts were this is only a part of the journey. You will and probably have heard me repeat over and over again, everything happens for a reason and it certainly does. When someone turns their back on you there is a reason. This reason doesn't always necessarily have to do with you either. We are all struggling things that the surface cannot see. Our friends and family only know of our struggles if we disclose the issue to them.
I watched a movie last night that challenged you to do what you would do if you only had 90 minutes to live, Who would you call? Who would you want to spend your time with? So often we take life and time for granted we say that we

have time to get back to that but do we? How do you know? You don't.

This thought caused me to make a decision that too much time has been wasted chasing something or a person. There should be small triumphs during the challenge. For instance, when you play a video game you level up. It takes time to win the game but you have small successes by reaching the next level. Same thing with work as well. You move up from position to position. What do you do when you are not leveling up? Do you re-strategize or reinvent your approach? Do we waste more time or move on? I personally move on, I would tell that person that I loved them one last time, but I wouldn't want a response and I would probably block the response, honestly. Not saying that action is right, by far. When you think of not having much time left, what decisions change. Do you chase that person or thing for the last 24 hours or do you send love and move on? If that thing or person you are pursuing, is not gaining any ground, reinvent your approach, try again. If still no success, remove it from your life. If something else pops up that must be done, focus on that and don't let it go. Strive hard and don't miss your level ups, this is your confirmation your on the right path. If it is a relationship or friendship that needs to be fixed, try to mend it, however, time is not guaranteed. Work on it, now!

YOLO.... that's the saying, right? You Only Live Once...
Brooke' s Thoughts

Let's dig into what this business is going to do and how it is going to run.

Go to your workbook to answer question 1-3 for Chapter 4.

The most important from these three questions is the last. We will begin with the first two as it will make it easier for us to answer the last. Please preliminarily answer these questions. You will add more details as we go thru the chapter.

Now that we know what your businesses focus is, let's discuss the product and/or services. Identify your main product(s) and/or service(s) your business plans to offer.

Go to your workbook to answer question 4 for Chapter 4.

Is there something else that you can include that can expand your customer base. For example, if your business sells health drinks have you considered health food. If you are running a laundromat, do you sell detergent and softener or folding services? This the area where you get to speak about your main focus but also consider your crazy add-ons that may be very instrumental in building your business. Limiting yourself can sometimes limit your customers. It is important to recognize these crazy add-ons and eventually analyze the value of them. If you can add something with a low cost but high return you have hit the jackpot.

Go to your workbook to answer question 5 for Chapter 4.

As you decide which add-ons you may want to add into your options. You will want to analyze cost and value of each add-on. The add-ons that are low in cost but can be sold for a high return are the ones you want to move to the top of the list. Sunglass Hut sells sunglasses but they also sell cleaner and kits.

Go to your workbook to answer question 6 for Chapter 4.

Now that you have identified your product who is going to have the highest interest. Some products will have kids and teens and maybe dads too. It is important to identify who will be the first group with interest. Then we need to know who is going to buy it for this group. Let's use drones as an example. Drones are a new technology that has sparked the interest of teen boys and men. Well for both of these groups the mom or wives are more than likely to buy it for them. The dads may also buy it for their sons because they have an interest. You may want to market this product with family items and entertainment products. You want the whole family to see the product together so the kids can ask their parents for it while they are all together. YouTube videos are also going to help this product make sales putting the customer into the seat of actually using this product drives the desire for it even more. If the mom is the decision maker she will receive additional pressure if the dad is into this product as well. When you are thinking marketing think about the entire process of the sale. This will help you decide your target market. Also, note that interest may need to be marketed to a certain group and sales to another group.

Go to your workbook to answer question 7-8 for Chapter 4.

If everybody is your answer, great, however targeting a specific client will build your business more efficiently. Most successful businesses started with a target market and then branched out. Let's look at the Gap brand. Gap has five different brands: GAP, Banana Republic, Old Navy, Athleta, and Intermix. Each store is marketed towards a different market. They all have a common cause a similar style of clothing, however price, style and quality is different in each brand. This is the way you must market your product you want your product to be specific to a need of your target market. Your advertisements are going to look like your consumer. You want your consumer to be able to visualize themselves with product creating a deep desire to have it immediately.

Go to your workbook to answer question 9 for Chapter 4.

After you specify your market. Write 10 things that individualize your market. This can include sex, style, quality, etc. These should be things that will allow your market to like your product or things that your market will like about the product. The options that would suit them best.

Go to your workbook to answer question 10 for Chapter 4.

When you think about your business name think of something that is going to be appealing to your target market more than current competition. The name or your business is your first impression. As we all know, first impressions can make or break a deal. For example, would you run to get ice cream from Poop Scoops Ice Cream? I personally wouldn't run to buy poop scoops. What comes to mind when you hear this name? Personally, dog poop comes to mind. I don't want dog poop ice cream.

Consider the impression when you decide your name. Your business name shouldn't also be so trendy that it will be old next week. Do you want a business for 3 yrs or 20 yrs? Your business name shouldn't grow old it should gain wisdom. For example, Pops Scoops sounds much better. Even Pop Scoops makes it sound cool but not too trendy.

    Consider your client when you are building your marketing plan. Look at others marketing plans and see what is missing and what you like. Include the things that you like and add the things that are missing for you as a consumer. Placing yourself in the consumer's shoes is the most important part of this process. It allows you to think about all the ways in which you would want to be catered to as a consumer. It also gives you an awareness of things that turn you off as well. List your turn-offs to make sure your business never does these things. As businesses grow they tend to become generic in product and services as they are trying to reach more and more people.

Starbucks, one of my favorite brands as stayed true to their customer service. They give you a personal experience every time you walk in. Writing your name on the cup just makes it personal each and every time. Along with your way of making your coffee to your liking.

Chapter 5

Financing your business

Didn't you just hate the teachers who gave you extra homework on a long weekend? But rather than not wanting you not to have fun, they were more concerned with increasing your capacity to understand the subject matter at hand. And they probably got more out of you than most of your other teachers. Life is that kind of teacher. Long weekend, short weekend, holiday, morning, noon or midnight, life is continuously teaching us lessons. And the biggest lesson we can learn is who we are. When we begin to understand who we are, we begin to draw on our potential. And just like that unrelenting, difficult teacher back in school, life can be the same. But once we realize that every living being has his or her unique and personal problems to deal with, and we are no different, we can welcome the opportunities we have to grow. Once we stop focusing on what others have or don't have and start to discover our own strengths and weaknesses, we can move on to a new level of understanding. We all think that there is some situation that only we have to deal with. You're right. Accept it, deal with it, and move on. Too often we try to avoid, and postpone, and ignore, the very thing that will set us free. We slow up just before we reach the finish line, we stop pushing when one more burst will get us over the hump. If we realized the power and potential we have within us, fear, doubt, and unbelief could not exist in our minds. Identify what you do well and capitalize on that. Look back and see what works best for you and utilize it. Look forward at your goals and desire and know that every obstacle you encounter is preparing you for success. Do your homework. Study who you are. - Blaine Group Moments

As an accountant the number one question I receive is, how can I afford to start my business. In conversation, many have told me that they will wait until they have the funds. Do you live check to check? If so, what is the likelihood of you having those needed funds? When is the last time you had 5k cash? That is a very low start-up. Many people don't have cash and you are not alone.

Thru this book I spoke about many ways do things on your own and at low cost. This is how you're going to start your business minimize the cost the best way possible. Eliminate all cost that you don't have to incur now. Make a list and list how the things you must pay for versus things you will eventually need to pay for. Itemize and add cost to each item. Look at each item and see if there is a free option. Look at each item and analyze the highest closet versus the lowest cost. Decide high cost is necessary to run the business or if it is just where you would like to be in the future.

Go to your workbook to answer question 1 for Chapter 5. Fill out the chart.

During the first year of business, many large purchases are made. Your business may require to buying a car, a building, or equipment that you will be able to amortize over the life of the item. These large expenses will not occur in the following years. Many businesses take a loss the first year, this is normal. I say loss and you think negative money, money can still be made, your loss is on your books. These items may be purchased with credit and paid over time. Once again don't dig your hole too deep. As a business grows, you should then increase benefits to the customer, then pay a little more for the basics.

Some businesses will need start-up funding. This is when you get creative. Option one, obtain funding from a lender. There are plenty of grants, lenders, etc. that are more than willing to help you start your business. The first step to acquiring funding you must have a business plan. This tells your audience, what you are doing, how you are going to make the money and how you will be able to pay a loan back.

Once your business plan is complete you will either need to have your current financials or a future cast created if the business is not running yet. You want to approach your lender with a business plan, financials, and credit worthiness. An EIN should be established for your company. The business needs to be incorporated and a bank account needs to be opened. If you choose not to incorporate your business you can set it up as a DBA, this, however, will require everything to be under your personal social security number.

Option two start small to show your audience that this business can make money. Businesses that are already operating tend to be more attractive to those providing the funding. Thru this book we have discussed ways to start this business with only what you have.

Go to your workbook to answer question 2 for Chapter 5.

Option three network, talk to fellow business owners and those that may have a similar or same service. You all are not in competition as you may cater to your client totally different. Network with other entrepreneurs, find banks in your area that cater to small businesses. Have you attended meetings and networking events of the professional organizations in your area? Professional organizations are excellent to grow your business. Most of them have many free events that non-members can attend. They also have the option for non-members to attend events for members with a small cost. The Chamber of Commerce and the small business administration are great places to start for business owners. Also look for professional organizations that cater to your area of expertise. The fee for most of these organizations is roughly $100- $200 per year. This is an excellent investment and can be claimed on your tax return.

Level Up! The Guide
How to turn your ideas into your business!

Go to your workbook to answer question 3-5 for Chapter 5.

Chapter 6

Intro to Incorporation

One of the most important parts of the golf swing takes place before you ever move the club. It's your setup. If your club face is not aligned squarely to your target, the ball won't go straight. If your feet are not set to allow the clubface to contact the ball at the proper angle, you will not produce the shot you want. If the ball is not in the proper location in your stance, your ball flight will be off course. In life set up is equally important. If you don't have your mind set squarely on your goal, you will vacillate and be distracted from your goal. You will be indecisive and not trust in your ability, your worthiness, your right to accomplish your goal. If you do not take care of your body, and it is not fit and able to support the activities necessary to accomplish your goals, you will not be able to maintain the effort necessary to turn your dream into reality. If your spirit is not positioned properly, if you are not determined, unrelenting, focused, and internally able to see, feel, and taste what you want, you will fall short. And we all fall short sometimes. But when you fall short don't quit, don't give up. Find your ball, find out where you are and accept yourself right there. Reaffirm your target, hold your head up, and make a firm decision to go after your goal, and make your swing, take action. In golf it doesn't matter where your playing partner's ball is, you can only play your ball, where it lays, you can only live your life from where you are. Pick your target, set your goals, dream your dreams, and visualize your shot, see yourself succeeding. - Blaine Group Moments

Let's talk incorporation. You have the option to incorporate as a single proprietor, LLC, partnership, or corporation. There are different benefits with each entity. Your job is to find which fits best for your business.

Incorporating your business is completed with your local state agency.

Go to your workbook to answer question 1-7 for Chapter 6.

Name of your business?

    The name of your business should be inviting to your target market. Make sure you carefully think about your business name and how it will cater to your market. Also, remember you can change it as well. When you start to brand your company you will not want to change it however if you decide the first name you choose is not the best name you can always place D.B.A. (doing business as) on necessary documents.

Purpose of business?

    The purpose of your business should encompass why you are running this business and what you hope to accomplish. Your business name should attract your potential clientele.

Industry of business?
    If you are unsure of the industry for your business, name 3 categories you think your business should fit into and then you can complete research when you look into marketing.

Owners and/or Partners?
    Do you have anyone in mind to help with the business? How many owners do you plan to have? Are you going to have a board? Who is going to help and what are they going to do? Have partners, what percentage of the profit will each partner receive? If your company has multiple owners, who will be the initial agent? When deciding to go into business with someone else there are a lot of factors that need to be addressed. The questions in the beginning only address a few. You must decide how active each partner must be in the business, you will

need to decide profit and loss splits. It's easy to say it will be 50- 50 when one person ends up running the facility while the other still has a 9-5. Decisions should be made with a neutral third party and a partnership agreement is strongly recommended when you are dealing with multiple owners. This can avoid future issues down the line.

    In making decisions about your partnership. Decisions about your business type should be addressed as well. Many small business owners usually incorporate under an LLC. This is the most popular of organization styles, however, it is not always the best choice for all businesses. I recommend consulting with your tax professional before making this decision. This way you are able to address tax liability pros and cons of each way to organize your company. Following is a short description of each organization. This description does not include all needed details to a make an informed decision as laws change from state to state. Please consult your tax professional for full advisement.

Visit www.blainelacar.com/levelup/corporations/types-of-corporations to download your free guide. Password is Types!

    The information in your workbook will help you file for your EIN and incorporate in your state. All the questions for this chapter must be answered and in detail. Be sure about your officers and your business status for tax purposes and make sure partnership agreements are written by a lawyer.

    To incorporate your business go to the website for the secretary of the state for the state your business's headquarters resides.

Visit www.blainelacar.com/levelup/corporations/secretary-of-state to obtain the information for your state. Password is SOS

Incorporating your business is not a part of your first steps. This is a part of your formative steps. If you have a t-shirt business and you are just starting, incorporation may not be on your priority list just yet.

Ok now that you have written the foundation of your business, how do you feel? Great, I hope.

To obtain your EIN go to the IRS website at www.IRS.gov. Search for Obtain EIN. Do not use any other website as you can do this yourself for free.

Level Up! The Guide
How to turn your ideas into your business!

Chapter 7

Wrap Up

Finding the Gold

Many motivational speakers speak about being optimistic and not letting people get you down. However, I know that this is much easier said than done. Today I want to give you a few steps to finding the gold in every instance in your life. When should you find the gold?
You should find the gold, whenever you are uneasy or unhappy about something. Once you realize this thing or event is bothering you it's time to make an assessment. You are making this assessment because we don't want this thing to bother us any longer than it should. Often worries can slow your progress down or

temporarily detour you. So to avoid the detour or the slow down, let's find the gold!

If you had $1000 and someone took $10. How much do you have? $990. Are you going to chase that person who took the $10? If not, then why do we spend more than 10 minutes on losses? I challenge you to take no more than 10 minutes on losses, no matter what it is.

Where do you find the gold?

You already possess the gold it's inside of you. You own it. Your personality is gold as you are unique in your own way. Your patience and endurance is gold as you have made it thru many trials and tribulations. Your mind is gold as although we tend to sometimes get off track it steers you back to your main focus. Take a moment and write down five things that make you, you. Then write down five more things you have that money can't buy. Then three more things you have that money has brought. You are a pretty wealthy person, huh. You are rich in gold and always have been! - Brooke's Thoughts

Level Up! The Guide
How to turn your ideas into your business!

One thing I have learned in my journey is if you don't make the first step, you go nowhere. I want you to know that I made a decision, to make the first step every day. Every day you make a first step you will gain something. Even if it is the door closing in your face you gained a lesson that pushes you closer to your goal. The longer you wait to make your first step the longer you sit in your dream.

You have found your gold! Now use it to your advantage! The longer you wait to start your business the more dust it collects on the shelf. I speak to people daily that want to start their business but don't have any idea as to where they should start. What can you do today to start your business? That was one of our first questions and since we are now at the end of this book. I want you to answer the question again. I hope that your answer has grown into a page of actions. List out your actions and begin today.

Level Up! The Guide
How to turn your ideas into your business!

Today is the day you start your business!

Author's Special Message for you!

Guess what! Thru this book we have covered all of the different aspects of your business plan. Make sure you answer all the questions in detail. I hope you have answered all of the questions in your notebook. Take your answers from your notebook and place them in a word document. I want to congratulate you not only for finishing the book and starting your business. You have also completed your business plan! Your answers to the questions are all you need for your business plan. You will also need financials if you plan to present this plan to investors and/or banks for funds.

If you are in need of financial statements please do not hesitate to contact my firm as we have accountants ready and available to fulfill your needs.

Go to www.blainelacar.com/consultation to schedule your consultation today!

Go to www.blainelacarassoc.com/levelup/templates to access your free business plan template. This is free to you for purchasing this book. The access code is LevelUp.

www.ingramcontent.com/pod-product-compliance
Lightning Source LLC
Chambersburg PA
CBHW050242230526
45470CB00005B/2076